THE STORY OF THE INDIANA PACERS

THE NBA: A HISTORY OF HOOPS

THE STORY OF THE INDIANA PACERS

NATE FRISCH

CREATIVE EDUCATION

Published by Creative Education
P.O. Box 227, Mankato, Minnesota 56002
Creative Education is an imprint of The Creative Company
www.thecreativecompany.us

Design and production by Blue Design
Art direction by Rita Marshall
Printed in the United States of America

Photographs by Corbis (Bettmann, Gary Coronado/
ZUMA Press, Steve Lipofsky), Getty Images (Andrew D.
Bernstein/NBAE, Nathaniel S. Butler/NBAE, Gary Cralle,
Tim DeFrisco, Ned Dishman/NBAE, George Gojkovich,
Ron Hoskins/NBAE, Heinz Kluetmeier/Sports Illustrated,
AJ Mast, Fernando Medina/NBAE, Layne Murdoch/NBAE,
NBA Photos/NBAE), Newscom (Ron Cortes/Philadelphia
Inquirer/MCT, Jim Rassol/ABACAUSA.COM, STEVE
SCHAEFER/AFP)

Library of Congress Cataloging-in-Publication Data
Frisch, Nate.
The story of the Indiana Pacers / Nate Frisch.
p. cm. — (The NBA: a history of hoops)
Includes index.
Summary: An informative narration of the Indiana Pacers
professional basketball team's history from its 1967
founding to today, spotlighting memorable players and
reliving dramatic events.
ISBN 978-1-60818-432-3
1. Indiana Pacers (Basketball team)—History—Juvenile
literature. I. Title.

GV885.52.I53F75 2014
796.323'640977252—dc23   2013038288

CCSS: RI.5.1, 2, 3, 8; RH.6-8.4, 5, 7

First Edition
9 8 7 6 5 4 3 2 1

Cover: Forward/guard Paul George
Page 2: Forward Jermaine O'Neal
Pages 4&5: Forward Danny Granger
Page 6: Forward/guard Paul George

TABLE OF CONTENTS

COURTSIDE STORIES

INTRODUCING…

UNCONVENTIONAL ORIGINS

MODERN INDIANAPOLIS BOASTS CHAMPIONSHIP TEAMS IN BOTH BASKETBALL AND FOOTBALL.

ROGER BROWN

n the American Midwest of the early 1800s, most cities were settled along major rivers, offering ease of transportation for people and goods. Indianapolis, Indiana, was an exception. The 1821 settlement lay along the Cumberland Road, the first federal highway in the United States and, at the time, the smoothest overland route from east to west. Decades later, railroad travel offered the most efficient means of getting to and from Indianapolis. With spurs connecting to cities such as Chicago, Detroit, Louisville, St. Louis, and Cleveland, Indianapolis earned the nickname "The Crossroads of America." The city kept pace with the automobile manufacturing craze by the turn of the 20th century, and then it cemented its unique motor car legacy when it introduced the Indianapolis 500 auto race in 1911.

However, the state of Indiana may be even better known for another sport—basketball. The term "Hoosier"

9

technically applies to any Indiana resident, but to many, it has become synonymous with basketball. This is largely thanks to the long, proud history of the Indiana University Hoosiers basketball program, which began in 1900, won the first of its five national titles in 1940, and typically featured homegrown talent. So when a new professional league, the American Basketball Association (ABA), was starting up in 1967, Indiana seemed an ideal host for one of the franchises. In a nod to the city's auto racing history, the Indianapolis-based team would be called the Pacers.

The Pacers and the ABA as a whole were taking a big risk. An older, larger league called the National Basketball Association (NBA) already had a fan base and employed most of the nation's best players. However, success was never in doubt in basketball-crazed Indiana, especially since the Pacers had no in-state competition from the NBA. When the Pacers took the floor for the first time on October 14, 1967, versus the Kentucky Colonels, an overflow crowd at the Indiana State Fair Coliseum watched Indiana race away with a 117–95 victory.

The Pacers would draw larger crowds than any other ABA team that first season despite being a middle-of-the-road club, record-

BOB NETOLICKY

CHAMPIONSHIP NUMBER ONE

After reaching the 1969 ABA Finals and losing to the Oakland Oaks, the Pacers were primed for a championship run in 1969–70. With center Mel Daniels and forwards Roger Brown and Bob Netolicky leading the way, the Pacers rolled to a 59–25 mark. Daniels was a rugged force in the middle on both offense and defense, but the Pacers' real strength was playing a fast-paced, high-scoring game. The best example of this occurred near the end of the regular season, when Indiana humiliated Pittsburgh, 177–135. In the 1970 playoffs, the Pacers were a runaway train. They defeated Carolina in a four-game sweep in the first round, and then routed Kentucky four games to one. There was no stopping the Pacers in the ABA Finals. The Los Angeles Stars had caught fire to advance to the championship series, and they rode the hot shooting of guard Mack Calvin to capture two wins in the series. But Indiana would not be denied. Brown poured in 45 points in Game 6 as the Pacers won 111–107 and celebrated championship number one.

ROGER BROWN

POSITION FORWARD / GUARD
HEIGHT 6-FOOT-5
PACERS SEASONS
1967–75

Roger Brown was one of the ABA's signature players as the league fought for respect in the shadow of the larger NBA. His slashing offensive style became the standard that many great players in later years would emulate, yet if a defender backed off Brown a couple of steps to neutralize his quickness, he would simply drain the outside shot. Brown's pro career never would have gotten off the ground if not for the ABA. In high school, he had been introduced to a known gambler. Even though there was no evidence that Brown had committed any wrongdoing, the association alone cost him dearly, as he was banned from playing college ball and shunned by the NBA. Welcomed by Indiana, he played on all three of the Pacers' ABA championship squads, was the franchise's all-time leading scorer among ABA players, and was a unanimous selection to the ABA's All-Time Team, as announced in 1997. "He was simply a great player as well as a great scorer," said Hall of Fame forward Rick Barry. "Roger could always make a big play when the game was on the line."

wise. Swingman Roger Brown and forward Bob Netolicky drew many of the cheers for their scoring and rebounding skills. Netolicky finished third in the entire league in field goal percentage, while Brown placed third in assists. Under head coach Larry Staverman, these budding stars led Indiana to a 38–40 record and into the playoffs. Unfortunately, the team was swept in the first round by acrobatic forward Connie Hawkins and the Pittsburgh Pipers.

In 1968, the Pacers boosted their talent pool by acquiring center Mel Daniels from the Minnesota Muskies and signing small but crafty guard Freddie Lewis. They also made a coaching change, promoting assistant Bobby "Slick" Leonard to the head coaching position. Leonard was a firebrand on the sidelines, a leader whose passion for the game quickly endeared him to the Indiana faithful. With new players and leadership, the 1968–69 Pacers displayed excellent offensive balance, and they assembled a 44–34 record before beating the Colonels in a thrilling seven-game playoff series. In that series, the Colonels built a three-games-to-one lead before the Pacers stormed back to win the last three contests. The Pacers followed that up by beating the Miami Floridians in the Eastern Division finals in five games. However, they fell just short of the league championship,

dropping the ABA Finals to the Oakland Oaks in five games.

That loss was only a temporary setback for the Pacers, though. Under Coach Leonard, they dominated the Eastern Division with a 59–25 record in 1969–70. Indiana's greatest strength remained its front line of Daniels, Brown, and Netolicky. While Brown was a slasher who could either drill jump shots or drive to the rim, the two bigger men utilized their height and muscle inside to crash the boards and sink close-range shots. Meanwhile, newcomer Billy Keller helped Lewis in the backcourt and became a fan favorite because of his short stature and accurate outside shooting.

The Pacers cruised through the 1970 playoffs, sweeping the Carolina Cougars, crushing the Colonels in a five-game Eastern Division finals series, and finally capturing the league title by toppling the Los Angeles Stars, four games to two, in the ABA Finals. Brown closed out the Finals in style, netting 45 points in a 111–107 Pacers victory. "Roger was just amazing for us," said Indiana general manager Mike Storen. "[NBA star] Oscar Robertson had told me how good Roger was, and he was even better than I thought he would be. He was a championship player."

INTRODUCING...

MEL DANIELS

POSITION CENTER
HEIGHT 6-FOOT-9
PACERS SEASONS
1968–74

The ABA was a league that featured numerous elite scorers. Outstanding defensive players were a rarity, especially in the low post. But superb defensive play helped center Mel Daniels earn the ABA's Most Valuable Player (MVP) award in 1969 and 1971, and his intimidating ability to block shots was a key ingredient in the Pacers' three league championships in 1970, 1972, and 1973. This was never more the case than in Game 5 of the 1972 ABA Finals between the Pacers and the New York Nets. With the series tied at two wins apiece, the Nets held the lead in the fourth quarter before Daniels changed the momentum with one play. New York star forward Rick Barry went in for what appeared to be an easy layup. But Daniels blocked Barry's shot into the hands of Pacers guard Freddie Lewis, who headed downcourt. Daniels likewise raced down the floor, took a return pass, dunked the ball while getting fouled, and made a free throw for a three-point play that propelled the Pacers toward a crucial 100–99 win. Two days later, Indiana won Game 6 and the ABA title.

15

FROM POWERHOUSE TO PEON

INDIANA NATIVE GEORGE McGINNIS SHARED 1974–75 ABA MVP HONORS WITH JULIUS ERVING.

The Pacers cemented their legacy as an ABA dynasty in the seasons that followed, winning two more titles in 1972 and 1973. The championships followed the 1971 acquisition of superstar forward George McGinnis. Nicknamed "The Baby Bull," McGinnis was a rare physical specimen who combined brute power with smooth moves. "McGinnis is so strong, you'd swear he weighs 300 pounds," said Virginia Squires forward Willie Wise. With McGinnis flexing his muscle, and with superb efforts from such other players as high-jumping forward Darnell Hillman and the reliable Netolicky, the Pacers beat the New York Nets in six games to win the 1972 title. Then they triumphed over the Colonels in seven games for the 1973 championship.

Unfortunately, while the Pacers were cruising (posting winning records again in 1973–74 and 1974–75), the ABA

GEORGE McGINNIS

POSITION FORWARD
HEIGHT 6-FOOT-8
PACERS SEASONS
1971–75, 1979–82

Known as "Big Mac" and "The Baby Bull," George McGinnis probably gained the most fame playing alongside star forward Julius Erving as a member of the Philadelphia 76ers, but he played his best and most effective basketball with the Pacers. McGinnis was an ABA All-Star in 1973, 1974, and 1975 and was a key contributor on two of the Pacers' three ABA championship teams. A power forward before the term was ever commonly used, McGinnis had incredible physical strength, yet he also displayed the speed and finesse of a much smaller man. He would often call for and get the ball down low, fake to his right, and then attack the basket by spinning left and scoring on an easy layup. Even if opponents knew the move was coming, they often could do little to slow him down. An outstanding football player during his high-school days, McGinnis loved getting physical with his opponents. "I think playing football really helped me," the big forward said. "I like going inside, knocking people around, and coming out with the ball."

was running out of money. In 1975, the league announced that its ninth season would be its last. Fortunately for the Pacers, the NBA invited Indiana and three other ABA franchises to join in 1976.

Although the NBA offered the Pacers new life, membership was not free. The Pacers, Nets, San Antonio Spurs, and Denver Nuggets each had to pay the NBA an entry fee of $3.2 million and would not be allowed to share in the league's television revenue for four years—stipulations that made adding new talent nearly impossible. Still, the Pacers persevered, finishing their first NBA season with a 36–46 mark and notching some notable victories. Perhaps most impressively, they beat the defending NBA champion Boston Celtics twice in January, including a 112–101 victory in Boston Garden.

he Pacers got a lift in the late 1970s from the scoring of swingman Billy Knight and the passing of guard Don Buse. Knight could fill up the nets from the outside or penetrate defenses and score inside, and he averaged 26.6 points per game in Indiana's first NBA season. He was quick to share the glory with Buse, who averaged 8.5 assists per game that year and

took more pleasure in setting up his teammates with the perfect pass than he did in scoring himself. "It's because of Buse that I'm having a great year," Knight told reporters. "He'll ask me if there's anything special I want to run. I tell him I'll do something, then I do it, and the ball comes right to me." Both Buse and Knight made the 1977 NBA All-Star Game, an achievement that would be the main highlight of the club's first four NBA seasons, as the Pacers posted losing records each year.

Indiana finally broke through in 1980–81, going 44–38 and, under head coach Jack McKinney, making the NBA playoffs for the first time. However, that resurgence was brief, as the team slipped to a 20–62 record in 1982–83 despite the best efforts of forward George Johnson and guard Butch Carter.

Pacers fans had reasons to be optimistic in 1985–86, as Indiana suited up such formidable scorers as center Herb Williams, guard Vern Fleming, and forwards Clark Kellogg and Wayman Tisdale. The Pacers at times appeared capable of putting the ball in the hoop almost at will, but leaky defense undermined their playoff prospects, and Indiana finished at the bottom of the Eastern Conference's Central Division with a 26–56 mark.

COURTSIDE STORIES

JOINING THE NBA

The ABA was not in a position of strength when the Pacers, Nuggets, Nets, and Spurs were allowed to join the NBA at the start of the 1976–77 season. Despite its exciting brand of basketball, the league was hurting for money, and the Pacers were probably in the weakest financial position of any of the teams set to make the merge. Some basketball fans were shocked that the Pacers were selected instead of the Kentucky Colonels, a team that was loaded with stars such as center Artis Gilmore. Many other fans, though, thought that—simply by virtue of dominating the ABA with three league championships—Indiana was deserving of new life in the NBA, star power and financial considerations notwithstanding. "I think when people think of the ABA, they think of the Pacers and the Nets, and I think that had a lot to do with them getting a chance to keep on going," said Julius Erving, a star forward in both the ABA and NBA. "They were such a dominant team. They earned that right to join the NBA."

PACERS MARKSMEN TAKE AIM

NBA ROOKIE OF THE YEAR CHUCK PERSON WAS A DEADEYE WITH RANGE AND ACCURACY.

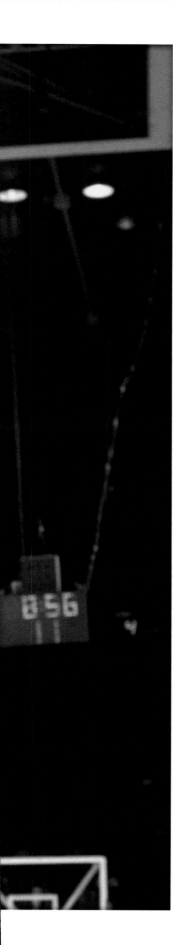

T he Pacers' outlook brightened in 1986–87 with the hiring of coach Jack Ramsay. Ramsay, who had led the Portland Trail Blazers to the 1977 NBA title, was known as one of the finest strategists in the league. He excelled at exploiting weaknesses of opposing teams and at covering up his own team's flaws by playing "help" defense, in which teammates could suddenly swap defensive assignments in the middle of the action.

Coach Ramsay had some talented players at his disposal in his first season in Indiana. Rookie forward Chuck "The Rifleman" Person provided brilliant outside shooting, Williams and center Steve Stipanovich led the charge in the frontcourt, and Tisdale supplied steady scoring off the bench. Of these players, Person was perhaps most valuable. In his first season out of Auburn University, the forward

CENTERS RIK SMITS (RIGHT) AND SHAQUILLE O'NEAL HAD A LONG-STANDING CONTEST.

brought a gunner's mentality to the court and netted an average of 18.8 points per game. Although Person sometimes showed a stubborn and cocky side, Coach Ramsay did all he could to coax the best out of him. Instead of yelling at the talented youngster, the coach employed a calmer, instructive approach. "There are ways to get your point across," Ramsay said. "And mine was never to scream and berate a player. There are plenty of coaches who have done that, and plenty who have failed."

Thanks to Ramsay's guidance and Person's marksmanship, the 1986–87 Pacers went 41–41 to earn a spot in the NBA playoffs for the first time in six years. Although they lost to the Atlanta Hawks, they scored big just weeks later. It was then, in the 1987 NBA Draft, that the Pacers found a player who would be the face

WAYMAN TISDALE'S TEAMMATES ADMIRED HIS POSITIVE ATTITUDE AND WORK ETHIC.

MILLER MAGIC IN THE GARDEN

Reggie Miller had a thing about playing the Knicks. After the Pacers had beaten the Magic and the Hawks in the first two rounds of the 1994 NBA playoffs, they squared off against the Knicks in the Eastern Conference finals. The clubs split the first four games before heading to New York's Madison Square Garden. Miller, Indiana's star guard, dropped 39 points on the Knicks in a 93–86 Game 5 win, including a phenomenal 25 in the fourth quarter. Still, New York went on to win the series. A year later, the Pacers met the Knicks in round two of the playoffs, and Miller stole Game 1 for Indiana single-handedly. With 16.4 seconds remaining, Indiana trailed 105–99. Miller then hit a three-point shot, stole New York's inbound pass, and drained another three-pointer. After the Knicks missed two free throws, Miller got the ball, was fouled, and made two free throws to seal an Indiana victory. Six games later, the Pacers won the series. "It was the Hatfields against the McCoys when we played the Knicks," Miller said, referencing the famous historical feud. "It was about doing anything possible to win."

"THERE ARE WAYS TO GET YOUR POINT ACROSS, AND MINE WAS NEVER TO SCREAM AND BERATE A PLAYER. THERE ARE PLENTY OF COACHES WHO HAVE DONE THAT, AND PLENTY WHO HAVE FAILED."

— COACH JACK RAMSAY

of their franchise for years to come: a sweet-shooting guard from the University of California, Los Angeles (UCLA) named Reggie Miller.

Miller was so skinny that some basketball scouts thought he was likely to get seriously injured amid the physical play of the NBA. But while the jug-eared guard was short on bulk, he was long on confidence and talent. Miller had been a big-time scorer at UCLA, earning renown as one of the best three-point shooters ever to play college basketball.

Miller was not dominant in his first NBA season, starting only 1 game and averaging 10 points per game in a reserve role. But his competitive nature was obvious. Miller raced tirelessly around the court, forcing defenders to chase him through screens, and launched scores of deadly outside shots with his remarkably quick release. As Person and Miller blazed away, the 1987–88 Pacers went 38–44.

In 1988–89, the Pacers slipped to 28–54. Although the finish was a disappointment, pieces were falling into place that would make the Pacers a contender again. The team had drafted a 7-foot-4 center from the Netherlands named Rik Smits in 1988, and although his play was initially awkward and at times timid, "The Dunkin' Dutchman" had offensive talent. Indiana had also made a midseason trade to obtain forward Detlef Schrempf, center LaSalle Thompson, and guard Randy Wittman. The Pacers appeared ready to make some noise.

INTRODUCING...
BOBBY "SLICK" LEONARD

COACH
PACERS SEASONS
1968–80

Slick Leonard was on the bench during the Pacers' run to dominance in the ABA. As an assistant to head coach Larry Staverman in the team's first season, Leonard observed firsthand that many players did not listen to Staverman's instructions. When he was promoted to head coach in 1968, Leonard quickly made clear that he was in command and that his instructions would be heeded. "You got the last guy fired," he told his players, "and I can promise you that you're not going to do that to me." Leonard was a disciplinarian who excelled at firing up his players, and he regularly engaged referees in screaming matches. Leonard's contortions often turned his expensive suits into rumpled, sweat-stained messes, earning him the ironic nickname of "Slick." Not all of Leonard's peers were big fans. Boston Celtics president and general manager Red Auerbach once called Leonard "a bad coach." But Leonard got the last laugh by leading the Pacers to three ABA titles. Through 2014, no one had ever coached the Pacers for more seasons than Leonard had.

EASTERN CONFERENCE BATTLES

FORWARD DALE DAVIS (RIGHT) BATTLED OPPOSING TEAMS' MOST PHYSICAL PLAYERS.

Under new coach Dick Versace (who had replaced Ramsay in 1988), Indiana earned a berth in the 1990 playoffs but lost to the Detroit Pistons in the first round. The Pacers then hovered around .500 the next three seasons, losing in the first round of the playoffs each time. In 1993, the Pacers put a proven winner, Larry Brown, on their bench. Brown, a longtime NBA coach, boasted an uncanny knack for looking at the talent on his roster and figuring out which types of schemes—offensively and defensively—best fit his players.

In 1993–94, Miller and Smits provided most of Indiana's offensive punch. Miller had emerged as one of the most dangerous scorers in the league, while Smits was a major force in the middle, developing a fine hook shot that became nearly unstoppable. Forwards Dale Davis and Derrick McKey, meanwhile, did most of the team's dirty

FINALLY, THE FINALS

The Pacers were given little chance by basketball experts when they met the Los Angeles Lakers in the 2000 NBA Finals. Los Angeles featured enormous center Shaquille O'Neal at the top of his game as well as up-and-coming star guard Kobe Bryant. Veteran guard Reggie Miller was Indiana's top weapon, and the Los Angeles native found an extra bit of motivation competing for an NBA championship versus his hometown team. Miller, center Rik Smits, guard Jalen Rose, and the rest of the Pacers lost the first two games of the series in Los Angeles. The Pacers' situation then became dire as the teams split the next two games in Indiana's Conseco Fieldhouse. In Game 5, Indiana played arguably the best game in franchise history, a 120–87 runaway victory. Rose notched 32 points, Miller netted 25, and the Pacers held Bryant to a mere 8 points. "It all came together for us for that one night," Rose said. "It was beautiful." Unfortunately for the Pacers, Game 6 proved to be the end of the line, as the Lakers won the game, 116–111, and the series.

"IT WILL ALWAYS HURT. THEY HAD A GREAT TEAM, AND I'M NOT DISPUTING THAT. BUT TO GET THAT CLOSE AND NOT WIN WILL ALWAYS BE WITH ALL OF US."

— REGGIE MILLER ON LOSING TO THE LAKERS IN THE NBA FINALS

work, hauling in rebounds and battling opposing teams' most physical players. Making valuable contributions coming off the bench were veteran guard Byron Scott and quick point guard Pooh Richardson.

The new-look Pacers went 47–35 and exorcised their demons by sweeping the Orlando Magic in their first postseason series victory since joining the NBA. The Pacers then beat the Hawks in round two to advance to the Eastern Conference finals. Although it battled the New York Knicks fiercely, Indiana lost Game 7 by a score of 94–90.

Indiana bounced back admirably from the bitter defeat, returning to the 1995 playoffs, sweeping the Hawks in the first round, and then exacting revenge on the Knicks in round two by out-dueling New York in another seven-game slugfest. The Pacers once again found themselves on the verge of their first NBA Finals, but they fell apart in the deciding Game 7 of the Eastern Conference finals versus the Magic, losing 105–81.

That loss would stick with the Pacers for several years as the team's upward momentum stalled. In 1999–2000, however, Indiana was

back in fighting form. By then, Coach Brown had been replaced by legendary NBA forward Larry Bird. Bird had been one of the greatest players in Indiana history, playing most of his college ball at Indiana State University before becoming a pro star with the Celtics. As Coach Bird stressed sound fundamentals and selfless play, the Pacers went 56–26 and were hitting their stride as the 2000 playoffs rolled around.

In the postseason, the Pacers crushed the Milwaukee Bucks and the Philadelphia 76ers to earn a spot in the Eastern Conference finals, where they once again faced the Knicks. Thanks to Miller's clutch play and the versatile efforts of forward Austin Croshere, Indiana topped New York in six games and advanced to the NBA Finals for the first time. There it met a Los Angeles Lakers team that featured star center Shaquille O'Neal and young guard Kobe Bryant. The Pacers managed to win two games— including a 120–87 blowout victory in Game 5— but were eventually overpowered. "It will always hurt," Miller said. "They had a great team, and I'm not disputing that. But to get that close and not win will always be with all of us."

INTRODUCING...

REGGIE MILLER

POSITION GUARD
HEIGHT 6-FOOT-7
PACERS SEASONS
1987–2005

A good argument could be made that, in the history of the NBA, there has never been a better outside shooter than Reggie Miller. As of 2014, Miller ranked second in the NBA in career 3-pointers made and had the 14th-highest points total in league history, an amazing achievement, considering that Miller was born with deformities in both hips that forced him to wear braces in order to learn to walk correctly. Miller built up his leg strength to compensate for that weakness and developed the devastating ability to shoot the ball in the blink of an eye against bigger and stronger opponents. He was a fearless shooter who was at his best in big games, and he loved the challenge of competing in the playoffs. "I have always thought of myself as a competitor and a fighter," Miller explained upon his retirement in 2005. "I wasn't the biggest, strongest, and I certainly wasn't the fastest. But I wanted the ball in my hands when the game was on the line. I was confident in my abilities, and my teammates were confident in me."

FLYING WITH BIRD

Many great basketball players make lousy coaches. They start running a practice, see that most players can't do things as well as they once did, and give up in frustration. Larry Bird proved an exception to that. The former Celtics great took over as the Pacers' head coach in 1997. Bird demanded discipline from his team and squeezed the most out of such stars as center Rik Smits and guards Reggie Miller and Chris Mullin. Bird had been known for his businesslike approach as a player, and he was just as straightforward as a coach, which endeared him to his players. "Larry treats us like men, and he expects us to act like professionals," Mullin explained after a practice in Bird's first season. "Basketball is not complicated, and Larry doesn't make it that way. All of us appreciate his approach." By the end of the 1997–98 season, the Pacers had posted an outstanding 58–24 record. Bird remained the Pacers' head coach for two more seasons, employing his great strategic and communication skills to lead Indiana all the way to the 2000 NBA Finals.

DESPITE THE PACERS'
LOSS, AUSTIN CROSHERE
EMERGED AS A STAR OF
THE 2000 FINALS.

WIPING
THE SLATE
CLEAN

THOUGH PLAGUED BY INJURY, GUARD T. J. FORD CONTRIBUTED SOLID OFFENSE IN THE LATE 2000s.

Typically, a team that has just reached the Finals sticks with a similar roster and strategy the following season. This was not the case in Indiana. Persistent foot problems forced Smits to retire, dependable point guard Mark Jackson left town, and the veteran Davis was traded to Portland for young forward Jermaine O'Neal. Futhermore, Bird stepped down as head coach, and one of his old playing rivals, Isiah Thomas, took the reins.

The loss of so many veterans gave young guns O'Neal and guard Jalen Rose the chance to shine. In 2000–01, Rose averaged 20.5 points per game, and O'Neal—who'd been considered a draft bust in Portland—tallied almost 13 points and 10 rebounds per contest, and he led the NBA in blocks. Indiana remained competitive but followed up a 41–41 regular season with a first-round playoffs exit.

THE PACERS COUNTED ON FORWARD TROY MURPHY FOR INSIDE SCORING AND STRONG REBOUNDING.

In 2001–02, Indiana swung a multiplayer trade that sent Rose to the Chicago Bulls for forward Ron Artest. The 6-foot-6 Artest was quick and heavily built. He was a capable scorer, but his bread and butter was suffocating defense, which helped Indiana make it to the postseason again. The Pacers split the first four games with the Nets. Game 5 was a double-overtime thriller in which Miller netted 31 points, but the Nets came away victorious.

The Pacers went 48–34 in 2002–03 but put up less of a fight in the playoffs. New coach Rick Carlisle was hired, and the Pacers' defense—headed up by Artest, O'Neal, and

pesky point guard Jamaal Tinsley—became one of the league's stingiest in 2003–04, as Indiana enjoyed a league-best 61–21 record. Miller credited both Carlisle and better teamwork for the improvement. "Rick really knew his stuff, and he was good at coming up with plays and matchups for us," Miller said. "At the same time, we were working together and making our shots." The solid coaching and teamwork carried Indiana past the Celtics and Miami Heat in the playoffs, but the Pistons spoiled the run in the Eastern Conference finals.

Trouble with the Pistons continued into the next season when an ugly early-season brawl

INTRODUCING...

DANNY GRANGER

POSITION FORWARD
HEIGHT 6-FOOT-8
PACERS SEASONS
2005–14

Coming out of high school, Danny Granger wasn't highly recruited and ended up at Bradley University—hardly a basketball powerhouse—in Peoria, Illinois. He later transferred to the more competitive University of New Mexico but still flew under the radar. In the 2005 NBA Draft, the lanky forward slipped to the 17th pick before being claimed by the Indiana Pacers. But after his first season, Granger was named to the NBA All-Rookie team. Three years later, he was averaging 25.8 points per game, earning the NBA Most Improved Player award and a spot in the All-Star Game. "He doesn't back down from any person or any challenge that he has faced, and he always plays hard," said Pacers coach Jim O'Brien. "When the intensity of the game bumps up a notch, he bumps it up another notch. If the game is physical, he's willing to get physical." Granger continued to advance his skills in the years that followed. The long, quick forward could strike from long range, hit pull-up jumpers off the dribble, use a soft touch in the lane, or attack the rim head-on. And as the star forward improved, so did the Pacers. The club went from mediocre in 2005–06 to Eastern Conference contender as of 2014.

AT 7-FOOT-2, CENTER ROY HIBBERT PROVED TO BE A VALUABLE ASSET UNDER THE BASKET.

INDIANA BASKETBALL
IN A NUTSHELL

If the decades of Indiana's history and appreciation of basketball had to be summed up in one small window of time, a seven-month period from 1986 to 1987 might be the best representation. On November 14, 1986, the movie *Hoosiers* was released. Influenced by actual events, the film depicted a 1950s high school basketball team from a tiny town in Indiana—a team whose underdog coach and players overcame numerous obstacles on their way to a dramatic state title. *Hoosiers* remains the quintessential hoops film to this day. Shifting from the silver screen to the hardwood, the Indiana University Hoosiers and legendary coach Bob Knight capped off a stellar 1986–87 season by navigating the National Collegiate Athletic Association (NCAA) tournament to capture the national championship. At the pro level, the Pacers weren't quite as successful that same season, but they did have the satisfaction of earning their first playoff appearance in six years. More importantly, it was on June 22, 1987, that the Pacers drafted guard Reggie Miller, who would spend his entire 18-year NBA career in Indiana and become the franchise's all-time greatest player.

during a game in Detroit resulted in major suspensions for Artest, O'Neal, and Pacers swingman Stephen Jackson. The handicapped Pacers still reached the postseason but exited at the hands of the infuriating Pistons once again. However, some of the bitterness between the clubs gave way to universal respect for 18-year veteran Reggie Miller, who had announced he would retire after the season. In his final game, the 39-year-old nailed 11 of 16 shots for 27 points, receiving a standing ovation from Indiana fans and Detroit players.

After dealing away Artest early in 2005–06, the Pacers went 41–41 and were quickly booted from the 2006 playoffs. They then missed each of the next four postseasons. By 2009–10, O'Neal had left, and young talent such as high-scoring forward Danny Granger and towering center Roy Hibbert stepped in to lead the offense. Partway through the 2010–11 campaign, 37-year-old Frank Vogel was appointed as head coach, and Indiana's 37–45 finish was good enough for a return to the playoffs. But the Pacers managed just 1 victory behind a 24-point, 10-rebound performance by Granger.

Vogel kept morale high going into 2011–12, and the Pacers' frontcourt gained potency with the signing of physical veteran forward David West and the emergence of second-year forward Paul George. West helped Hibbert battle down low, while Granger and George used their athleticism and shooting strokes to attack from all angles. Indiana kept its foot on the gas in the postseason, blowing past Orlando in the opening round. But then they ran into an ultra-talented Miami team who ousted the Pacers on their way to the NBA championship. Indiana was left to ponder the missed opportunity. "We just didn't have enough yet," Vogel said, "but we'll be back."

The Pacers would be back without Granger, who missed all but five games of the 2012–13 season with a knee injury. Fortunately, George filled his shoes with an All-Star season of his own, West and Hibbert remained tough, and young guards George Hill and Lance Stephenson had their best seasons yet. The club rallied to top the Central Division, and then bounced both the Hawks and the Knicks on its way to the Eastern Conference finals. When Indiana faced Miami once again, the teams traded victories up to the decisive Game 7, where the Heat proved too hot to handle, winning 99–76. Even so, a bright future remained in Indiana. "The great thing is we're a young team, and we are past the building stage," George said after the game. "This is really our first year tasting success. The rate we are going, we will see championships soon."

The following season, the team raced to its best start in franchise history (11–1) behind All-Stars George and Hibbert. Granger was traded to the Clippers as the Pacers topped the Eastern Conference. In a conference finals rematch with the Heat, Miami again came out on top, and Indiana was left to consider its options going into 2014–15.

The Indiana Pacers may not have followed the conventional route to the NBA, but they have been successful nonetheless. Over the years, Indiana has developed a rich history and love of basketball, and superstars such as Reggie Miller have given hoops-crazed fans plenty to cheer about. Today's Pacers want to accomplish even more and obtain the last missing piece from the Hoosier State's great basketball legacy—an NBA title.

IN THE 2012–13 SEASON, SCRAPPY PLAY GARNERED DAVID WEST 69 BLOCKED SHOTS AND 74 STEALS.

INDEX